Ginger

Activity Book 4

Early Start Edition – Neubearbeitung
Lehrwerk für Englisch ab Klasse 1

Überarbeitet von
Ulrike Kraaz und
Christel Simon

auf der Grundlage
der Ausgaben von
Kerstin Caspari-Grote,
Ina Grandt,
Birgit Hollbrügge,
Ulrike Kraaz,
Claudia Neuber,
Christel Simon
und Ines Völtz

Cornelsen

Contents

Symbols

read	listen to the CD (CD 1.24)	act out	point
talk	draw	tick	colour in
write	cut	number	listen

Travelling the world

1 Read the words. Point to the countries.

2 Write the words. **3** Colour in the flags.

Australia • Canada • Great Britain • India • South Africa • the USA

___________ ___________ ___________

___________ ___________ ___________

Ländernamen lesen, auf die entsprechenden Länder auf der Karte zeigen, die Wörter schreiben und die Landesflaggen der Schiffsmitglieder sowie die eigene Heimatflagge ausmalen ▸ S. 110

Ginger in London

A map of London

1 Talk about the map.

2 Read and write the words.

3 Write the sentences

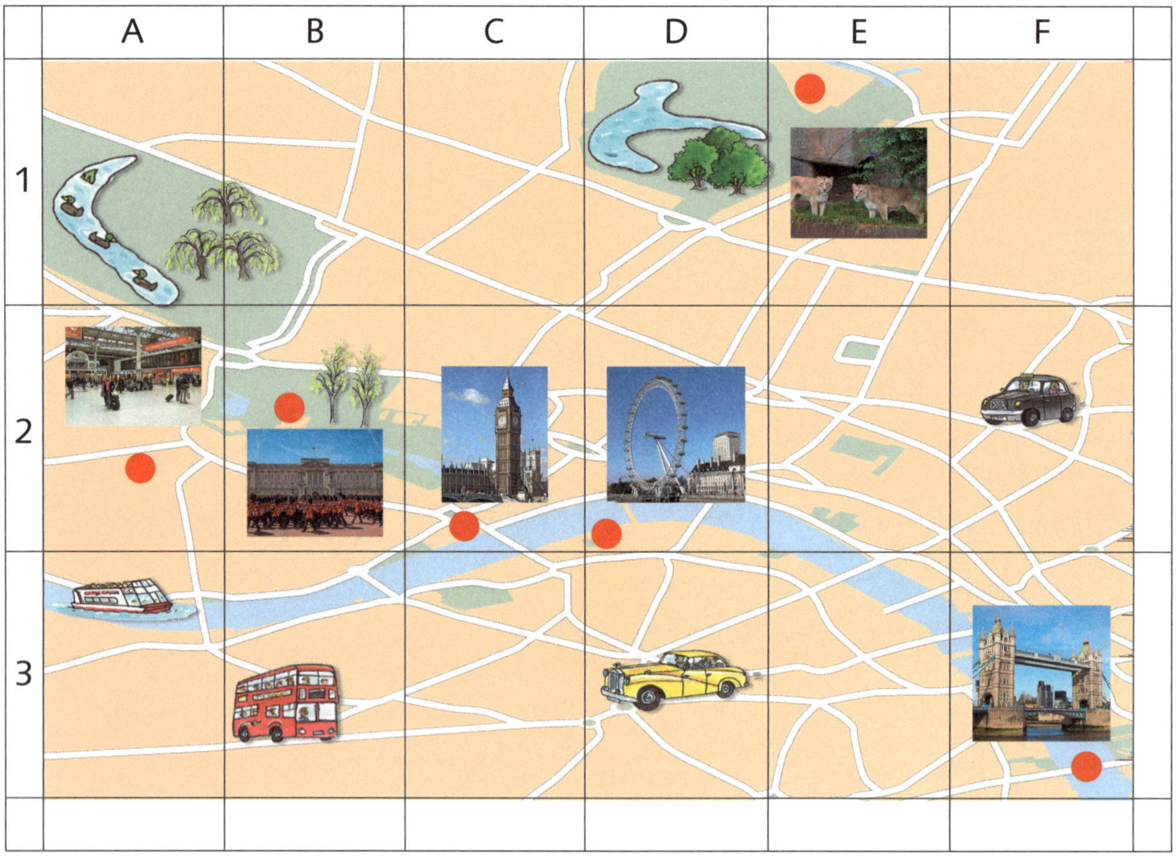

Big • Bridge • London • Palace • Station • Zoo

Buckingham ____________ : B2

Tower ____________ : ______

the ____________ Eye: ______

London ____________ : ______

Victoria ____________ : ______

____________ Ben: ______

I'd like to go to ____________________ .

I'd like to go to ____________________ .

And you? I'd ________________________________ .

Über den Stadtplan von London sprechen, die Namen der Sehenswürdigkeiten vervollständigen und aufschreiben, in welchen Planquadraten sie liegen, Sätze ergänzen ▸ S. 116

Let's go to London Zoo

1 Read the text.

CD 1.9 **2** Listen to the CD. Write the numbers.

1	Dennis:	Let's go to London Zoo.	
	Dennis:	I'm ten. Why?	
	Dennis:	Let's go by bus. It's a lot of fun.	
	Dennis:	Oh, I see. There's bus number 274 to London Zoo.	
4	Ellen:	How old are you?	
2	Ellen:	By underground or by bus?	
	Ellen:	Children under 11 travel free.	
	Ellen:	Great. Let's go and meet Ginger.	

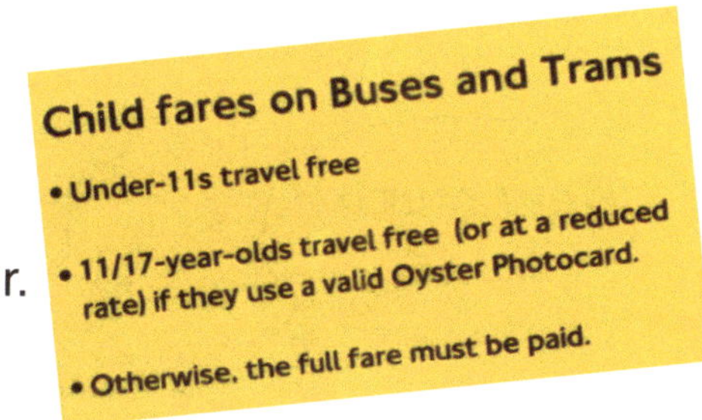

3 Read. Write the words.

bus stop • ticket machine • map of the zoo • underground

____

____

____

____

____

____

Einen Text lesen, einen Dialog verstehen und Sätze in der entsprechenden Reihenfolge nummerieren, Abbildungen beschriften ▸ S. 119/120

How much is it?

1 Talk about the pictures. **2** Read. Talk and write.

How much is a ticket for London Zoo?

The ticket is ________________.

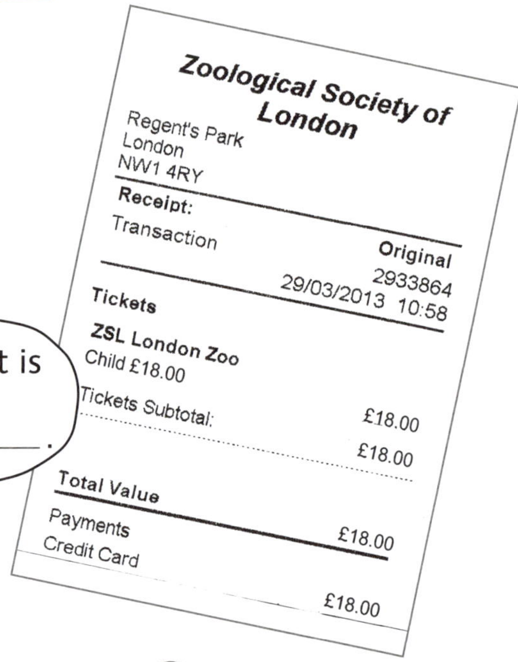
Zoological Society of London
Regent's Park
London
NW1 4RY

Receipt:	
Transaction	**Original**
	2933864
	29/03/2013 10:58
Tickets	
ZSL London Zoo	
Child £18.00	
Tickets Subtotal:	£18.00
	£18.00
Total Value	
Payments	£18.00
Credit Card	
	£18.00

How much is ...?

The sandwich is ________________.

The book ____________ ________________.

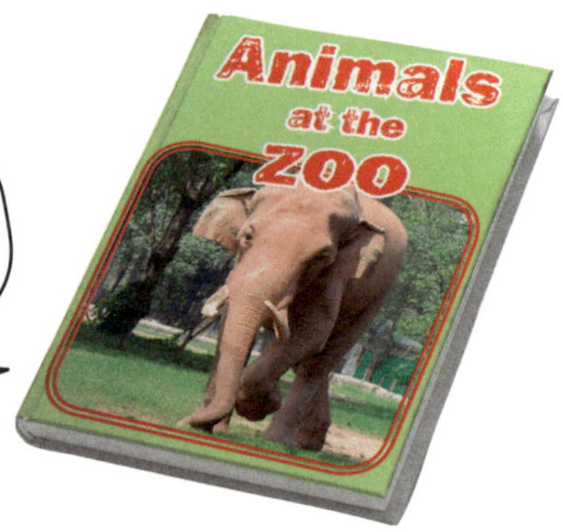

The T-shirt ____________ ________________.

Über die Abbildungen sprechen, sagen und in den Sprechblasen ergänzen, wie viel etwas kostet ▸ S. 120

At the zoo

1 Read and write more words. ✓ **2** Tick.

	big	dangerous	funny	small		
bears						
crocodiles						
elephants						
lions						
monkeys						
parrots						
snakes						

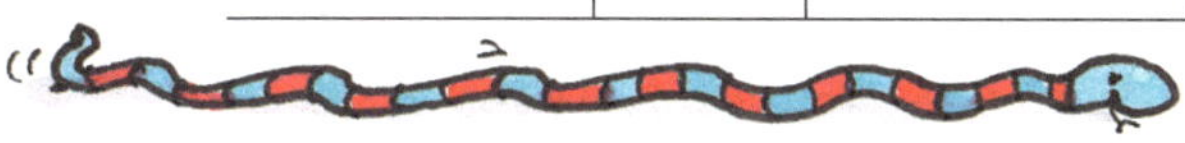

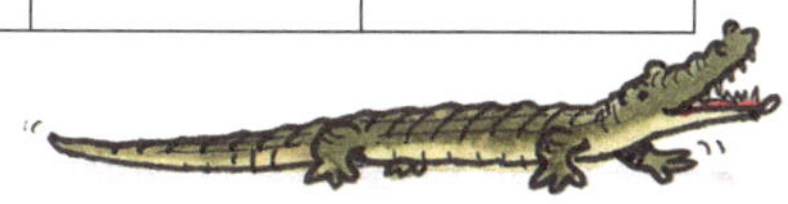

3 Write about the animals.

Bears are big and dangerous. ______________________________

____

____

____

4 Write the words. Number the pictures.

Boo • cat • London Zoo • rat

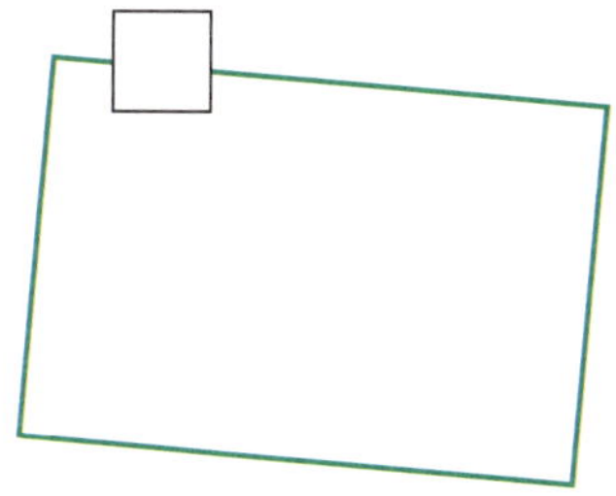

1 There once was a boa named __________.

2 She lived in the big __________.

3 ______ wanted a __________,

4 And so did a ______.

5 So ______ had to eat the ______, too.

Angaben in der Tabelle lesen und ergänzen, über die Eigenschaften von Tieren sprechen und schreiben; einen Limerick vervollständigen und die letzte Zeile zeichnerisch darstellen ▸ S. 122,124

Animals at the zoo

CD 1.13

1 Listen. Write the names.

2 Read. Write the sentences.

1. Jim is touching Bob's ________________.
2. Jim is touching ________________ ________________.
3. ________________ ________________.
4. ________________ ________________.
5. ________________ ________________.
6. ________________ ________________.

arm • ear • foot • head • knee • nose • shoulder

3 Write about the animals.

bear • crocodile • elephant • lion • monkey •
is climbing a tree • is drinking • is eating • is playing • is sleeping

1. A monkey ________________.
2. ________________.
3. ________________.
4. ________________.
5. ________________.

Einen Hörtext verstehen, Namen einsetzen und Sätze vervollständigen und schreiben; aufschreiben, was die Zootiere gerade tun ▸ S. 126

Dick Whittington

boy • ~~cat~~ • girl • man • queen • shoe • town

1 Read the words. Write the sentences.

big
(hungry)
dangerous

It's a hungry cat ______.

tired
sad
angry

He's a ______ ______.

strong
poor
funny

She's a ______ ______.

rich
poor
sad

She's a ______.

black
old
small

It's an ______.

angry
hungry
happy

He's a ______.

big
small
dangerous

It's a ______.

2 Draw. Talk.

Is there a rat on / in / under / behind the bed?

Yes, there is. / No, there isn't.

room 1

room 2

Wörter lesen, passende Adjektive einkreisen und Sätze ergänzen;
Ratten in *room 1* zeichnen und sich gegenseitig fragen, wo diese sich befinden ▸ S. 128, 131

A lot of holes

1 Talk about the pictures.

2 Read. Write the sentences.

dress • hat • pullover • shirt • skirt • shoe • sock

There's Alice. She has got a hole in her ______________________.

There's Dick. He has got a hole in his ______________________.

There's Dick. __________ has got a hole in ______________________.

There's Alice. __________ has got a ______________________.

There's Alice. ______________________ ______________________.

______________________ ______________________.

Über die Bilder sprechen, Wörter lesen und Sätze vervollständigen ▸ S. 130

Portfolio: A postcard from London

1 Talk. Read. **2** Write. **3** Draw.

Greetings from

LONDON!

Dear Grandma,

How are you? I'm in London with my friends.
Here's a picture of the London Eye. You can see London from the top. It's great!

See you on Friday.

Love, Emma

By air mail
Par avion

To

Über die Abbildungen sprechen, die Postkarte lesen,
eine eigene Postkarte aus London schreiben und gestalten ▸ S. 117/118

Was ich dazugelernt habe

Datum: ____________

Zeige jetzt noch einmal, was du kannst.
Ich fand die Aufgabe: ☺ leicht 😐 mittel ☹ schwer

◯ **1** Ich habe diese Lieder gesungen und den Limerick aufgesagt:
The wheels on the bus ☐ There's a hole in my sock ☐
Animals ☐ A boa named Boo ☐

◯ **2** Ich habe (Name) ____________________ gesagt,
wie die Sehenswürdigkeiten zu nummerieren sind.

Number 1 is ...

 ☐  ☐  ☐  ☐  ☐  ☐

◯ **3** Ich habe (Name) ____________________ gesagt, wie viel
das T-Shirt kostet.

◯ **4** Ich kann die Busnummern lesen und die Zahlen aufschreiben:

two hundred and seventy-four: ________ twenty-three: ________
five hundred and fifty-nine: ________ forty-six: ________

◯ **5** Ich kenne die englischen Wörter für Tiere und habe sie
(Name) ____________________ aufgezählt. Es sind ________ (Anzahl).
Ich habe gesagt, zu welchen Zootieren ich gern gehen würde. ☐

I'd like to go to the ...

◯ **6** Ich habe (Name) ____________________ gesagt, welche Eigenschaft
zu jedem Bild passt und kann die Wörter auch aufschreiben.

____

What's from the USA?

1 Tick the pictures and say the sentences.

… is from the USA.

… isn't from the USA.

1

☐

2

☐

3

☐

4

☐

5

☐

6

☐

7
☐

cap • dollar • elephant • flag • hamburger • Queen

2 Read the words. Write the sentences.

The ______________________________ is from the USA.

The ______________________________ isn't from the USA.

____.

____.

____.

____.

____.

Let's go for a picnic

There's …

There are …

1 Talk about the picture. Read the words.

CD 1.20

2 Listen. Tick.

apples • apple juice • bananas • cheese • cornflakes • cookies • eggs • ham • jam • milk • oranges • orange juice • peanut butter sandwiches • tomatoes • water

3 What's in your picnic basket? Write.

There's …
There are …
I've got …

Über eine Abbildung sprechen, Wörter lesen; einen Hörtext verstehen, Lebensmittel dementsprechend abhaken; aufschreiben, was man zum Picknick mitnehmen möchte ▸ S. 141/142

Let's fly a kite

1 Write the sentences. **2** Read with a partner.

~~collect seashells~~ • fly a kite • have a picnic • make a sandcastle • play with the beach ball • swim in the sea

1  Come on, Ginger.

Let's collect seashells.

2  Come on, Ginger.

Let's ______________________

______________________.

3  Come ______________________.

____

______________________.

4  ______________________.

______________________.

5  ______________________.

______________________.

6  ______________________.

____

____

______________________.

Captain Blue-Eyes and the pirates

123 **1** Number the speech bubbles. Read with partners.

8 Help! I can't swim!

Ha! Ha! Good luck, Captain Blue-Eyes! ☐

Now it's mine. ☐

Throw Captain Blue-Eyes to the sharks. ☐

Help! Pirates! ☐

1 Stop, Captain Blue-Eyes!

☐ Give me that treasure chest, Captain Blue-Eyes!

It's my treasure chest! ☐

2 Write the sentences. Read with partners.

3 Act out.

Pirate 1: Stop ______

Captain: ______

Pirate 2: Give me that treasure chest,
Captain Blue-Eyes.

Captain: ______

Pirate 3: ______

Pirate 2: Throw ______
______

Pirates: ______
______

Captain: ______

Sätze eines Dialogs in der richtigen Reihenfolge nummerieren, aufschreiben, mit verteilten Rollen lesen und die Szene anschließend vorspielen ▸ S.147/148

Cleaning up

1 Talk about the picture. Number.

It's in / on / under / behind …
What is it?

2 Read and write the words.

apple • basket • beach towel • blue bottle • book • glass • green bottle • ~~jack-o'-lantern~~ • kite • ~~magazine~~ • paper • paper cup • paper towel • postcard • radio • skateboard • sock • ~~white bottle~~

Rubbish	Glass	Paper
	white bottle	magazine
jack-o'-lantern		

Sagen, wo sich die Gegenstände auf dem Bild befinden und diese nach Ansage nummerieren;
Wörter lesen, Themenfeldern zuordnen und aufschreiben ▸ S. 152

Sports in the USA

123 **1** Read and number the words.

basketball ☐ football ☐ baseball ☐ volleyball ☐

American football ☐ badminton 1 table tennis ☐

2 Draw the pictures. Write the words.

basketball	table tennis	football	football	table tennis	
volleyball	basketball	table tennis	volleyball	basketball	
badminton	American football	baseball	American football	volleyball	
American football	football	basketball	table tennis	badminton	

3 Write sentences.

Jack can play ______________________ but he can't play

____.

____

____.

And you? I ____

____.

Bälle den entsprechenden Sportarten zuordnen und entsprechend nummerieren; logische Reihen fortsetzen; schreiben, welche Sportart jemand beherrscht bzw. nicht beherrscht ▸ S. 154

Portfolio: This is from the USA

1 Glue or draw pictures.

2 Write words or sentences.

Was ich dazugelernt habe

Datum: ____________________

Zeige jetzt noch einmal, was du kannst.
Ich fand die Aufgabe: ☺ leicht 😐 mittel ☹ schwer

◯ **1** Ich habe dieses Lied gesungen, diesen Rap gesprochen und den Zungenbrecher aufgesagt:
Beach ball boogie ☐ Pick it up ☐ I see seashells ☐

◯ **2** Ich habe (Name) ____________________ gesagt, was ich für einen Strandtag einpacke. ☐
Ich kann einiges davon auch aufschreiben: ____________________
____

◯ **3** (Name) ____________________ und ich haben uns gegenseitig vorgeschlagen, was wir am Strand machen könnten. Manchen Vorschlägen habe ich zugestimmt ☑, manche habe ich abgelehnt ☒.

 ☐  ☐  ☐  ☐  ☐  ☐

◯ **4** Ich habe mit (Namen) ____________________
die Filmszene „Captain Blue-Eyes and the pirates" gespielt. ☐

◯ **5** Ich habe (Name) ____________________ gesagt, wo sich die Gegenstände am Strand befinden.

 ☐  ☐  ☐  ☐  ☐  ☐

◯ **6** Ich habe (Name) ____________________ gesagt, welche Ballsportarten ich beherrsche ☑ und welche nicht ☒.

basketball ☐ football ☐ table tennis ☐ badminton ☐ volleyball ☐ baseball ☐

Going to Canada

city • lake • mountain • river • sea

CD 1.32–1.37 123 **1** Listen. Number.

2 Write.

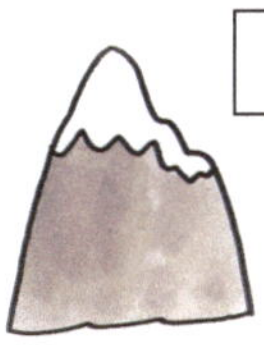 ☐

 ☐

 ☐

Vancouver

 ☐

 ☐

Calgary

 ☐

1 ____________ 2 ____________ 3 ____________

4 ____________ 5 ____________ 6 ____________

123 **3** Read the text. Number the English sentences.

1. Sarah will wissen, wie es ihrem Opa geht.
2. Sie sagt, dass es ihr gut geht.
3. Sie schreibt, dass sie in den Rocky Mountains zelten gehen wollen.
4. Sie fragt, ob ihr Opa mitkommen kann.
5. Sie schreibt: „Bitte komm mit!“
6. Zum Schluss schreibt sie: „Liebe Grüße, Sarah“.

☐ Can you come?

1 How are you?

☐ I'm fine.

☐ Love, Sarah

☐ Please come!

☐ We want to go camping in the Rocky Mountains.

4 Write Sarah's letter.

Dear ____________

____

____

____

____

____

Einen Hörtext verstehen, Abbildungen entsprechend nummerieren und Wörter schreiben; Sätze in die richtige Reihenfolge bringen; einen Brief nach Vorlage schreiben ▸ S. 163/164

At the camping store

CD 1.42

1 Listen to the CD. Read the dialogue.

Shop assistant: Can I help you?
Captain Storm: Yes, please. I'd like a sleeping bag.
Shop assistant: Here's a nice sleeping bag.
Captain Storm: How much is it?
Shop assistant: It's 45 dollars.
Captain Storm: OK, I'll take it. 45 dollars – here you are.
Shop assistant: Thank you. Here's your sleeping bag.
Captain Storm: Thank you.

2 Write.

I'd like ... a pocket knife • a rucksack • a sleeping bag • a tent • a torch • a water bottle

I'd like ______________ ______________ ______________

______________. ______________. ______________.

3 Write the sentences.

Can I help you?

Yes, please. I'd like ...

Shop assistant: Can ______________.
______________: Yes, please. I'd like a ______________.
Shop assistant: Here's ______________.
______________: ______________.
Shop assistant: ______________.
______________: OK, ______________.
Shop assistant: Thank you. ______________.
______________: ______________.

Einen Einkaufsdialog hören und lesen; Sätze schreiben; einen Dialog vervollständigen ▸ S. 166

Buffalo Camp

1 Talk about the picture.

2 Listen and point.

3 Read the sentences.

Sarah's grandpa is in the teepee with the fish on it.
Sarah is in the teepee next to her grandpa.
Sarah's mum is in the teepee with the eagle on it.
Lizzy is in her mother's teepee.
Eric is in his mother's teepee.
Sarah's dad is in the teepee with the sheep on it.
Ginger is in front of Sarah's teepee.

4 Look at the teepees. Write the names.

Ein Bild beschreiben, Aussagen verstehen und auf die genannten Dinge im Bild zeigen; Aussagen lesen und verstehen, die Tipis mit Namen beschriften ▸ S. 167/168

Animal tracks

1 Talk about the picture.

2 Write and read the sentences.

behind • in	grass • river • rock • tent • trees	bear • beaver • goose • moose • mouse

1 There's an animal behind the trees. It's a bear.

2 There's an animal ______________________________.

It's a ______________________________.

3 There's an ______________________________.

______________________________.

4 ______________________________.

______________________________.

5 ______________________________.

______________________________.

And where's Ginger? ______________________________.

Ein Bild beschreiben, Sätze vervollständigen, schreiben und lesen ▸ S.170

Portfolio: My birthday month

1 Glue your animal in the frame. Write about your birthday month.

My birthday is in ________________________.

My animal is the ________________________.

2 Write about your family or friends.

____

____

____

Über Geburtsmonate und die ihnen zugeordneten Tiere sprechen und schreiben ▸ S. 172

Was ich dazugelernt habe

Datum: ____________

Zeige jetzt noch einmal, was du kannst.

Ich fand die Aufgabe: ☺ leicht   😐 mittel   ☹ schwer

○ **1** Ich habe das Lied gesungen und den Chant gesprochen:

Camping song ☐   I'm the fastest ☐

○ **2** Ich habe (Name) ____________ gesagt, welche Dinge ich zum Camping mitnehme. ☐

Ich kann einige davon auch aufschreiben: ____________

____

○ **3** Ich habe mit (Name) ____________ „At the camping store“ gelesen (Pupil's Book, S. 16).

Wir haben uns mit den Rollen abgewechselt. ☐

○ **4** Ich habe (Name) ____________ die Namen von ____________ Tieren genannt, die in Kanada leben und gesagt, welches mein Lieblingstier ist. ☐   Ich kann es auch aufschreiben:

My favourite animal is the ____________.

○ **5** Ich kann Schneespuren erkennen und habe (Name) ____________ gesagt, von welchem Tier sie stammen. ☐

Ich kann die Tierwörter auch aufschreiben:

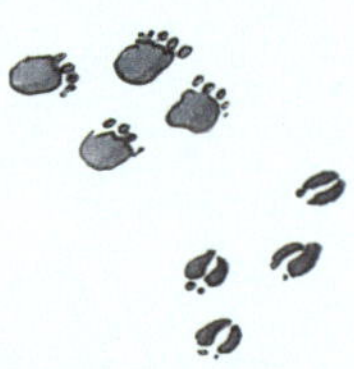

____

____

____

____

○ **6** Ich habe (Name) ____________ die Monatsnamen auf Englisch gesagt. ☐   Ich kann aufschreiben, in welchem Monat mein Geburtstag ist: ____________.

On the train

1 Talk about the picture. **2** Read and complete the chant.

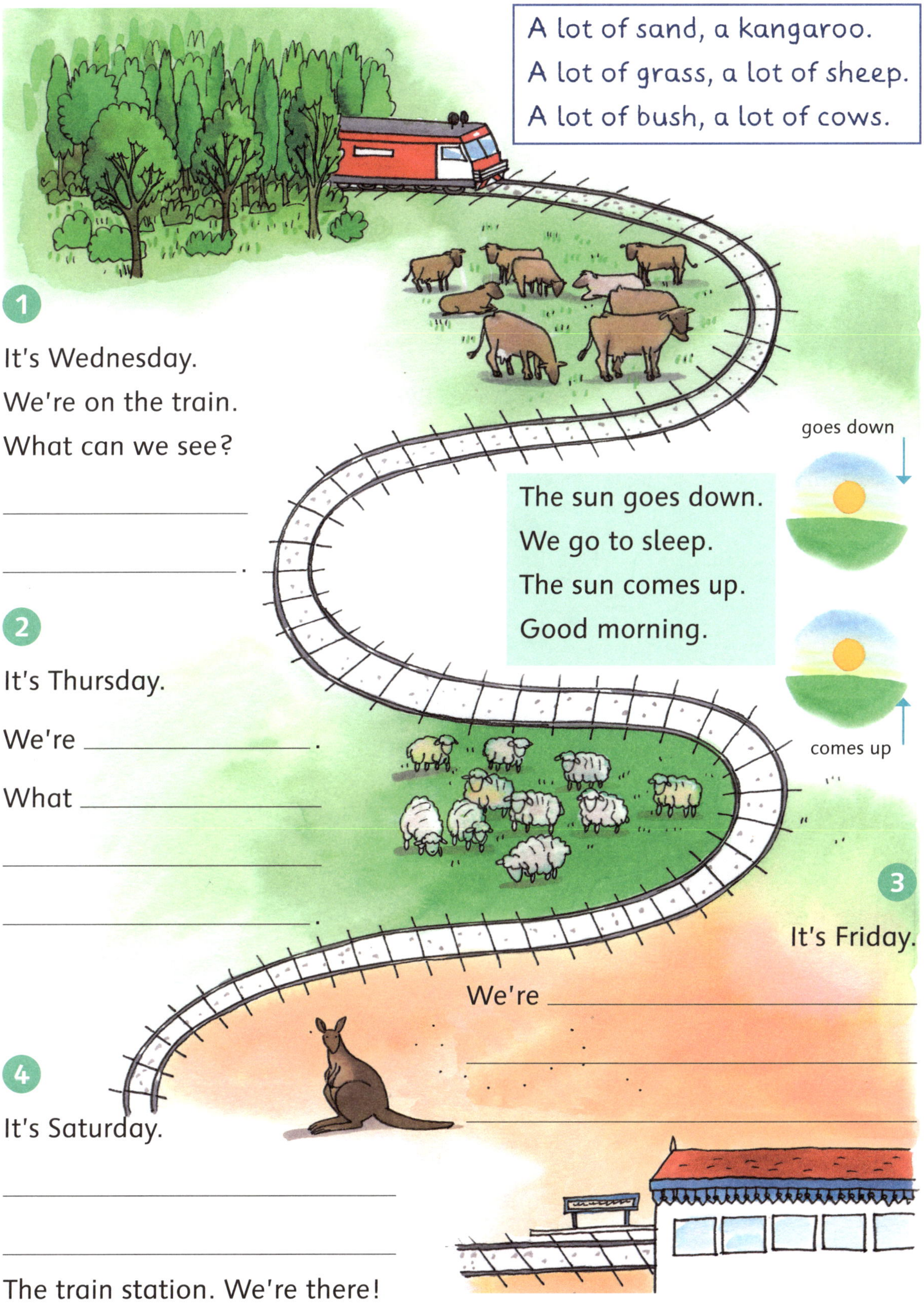

A lot of sand, a kangaroo.
A lot of grass, a lot of sheep.
A lot of bush, a lot of cows.

1

It's Wednesday.
We're on the train.
What can we see?

____

____________________.

The sun goes down.
We go to sleep.
The sun comes up.
Good morning.

2

It's Thursday.

We're ____________________.

What ____________________

____

____________________.

3

It's Friday.

We're ____________________

____

____

4

It's Saturday.

____

____

The train station. We're there!

Pets and animals on John's farm

123 **1** Number the animals. Talk.

1 budgie • 2 cat • 3 cow • 4 dog • 5 guinea pig • 6 hamster • 7 kangaroo • 8 koala • 9 rabbit • 10 sheep

2 Complete and read the sentences.

Ben

Have you got a pet?

Yes, I have. I've got a ________________.

Jenny

Yes, ________________.
I've got a ________________.

Paul Nick

Yes, ________________.
________________.

Jenny has got a ________________________________.

Paul ________________________________.

Nick ________________________________.

Sophie from Australia ________________________________.

Tom, her brother, ________________________________.

Emma, her sister, ________________________________.

What about you?
Have you got a pet?

Yes, I have. I've got …
No, I haven't./ I'd like to have …

____

____

Die Tierabbildungen entsprechend der *word bank* nummerieren und benennen; Sätze vervollständigen und lesen; aufschreiben, ob man ein Haustier hat ▸ S.186

Not now, Mum

1 Read. Write the sentences.

clean the birdcage • feed the dog • wash the cat's bowl

I'm playing a computer game.
I'm reading a comic.
I'm watching a DVD.

Please ______________________ .

______________________ .

______________________ .

Tom

Not now, Mum.

______________________ .

Emma

Not now, Dad.

______________________ .

Sophie

Not now, Mum.

______________________ .

2 Write a dialogue with a partner.

3 Act out.

______________ : Please ______________________
(Name)
______________ : Not now, ______________________
______________ : What are you doing?
______________ : ______________________
______________ : Come on, ____________ Please ____________
____
______________ : All right, ______________________

Kangaroo shoe

1 Read the sentences. Do the activities.

1. Draw an old shoe in the two green boxes.
2. Colour the shoes blue.
3. Read the words in the box. | foot • kangaroo • shoe • tired |
4. Write the missing words in the rhyme.
5. Underline the word zoo.
6. Tick the animals that can hop around:

dog ☐ rabbit ☐ cow ☐ frog ☐ kangaroo ☐

2 Read the rhyme.

Rhyme

A  ____________ on her way to the zoo

Is wearing a very old  ________ .

Only one  ____________ on the ground

The kangaroo is  ____________ of hopping around.

She is looking for another  ________ .

You'd better help this  ____________ !

Arbeitsanweisungen lesen, verstehen und ausführen, den Reim vervollständigen und lesen ▸ S. 193/194

Portfolio: My day

1 Write about your day. Draw the hands on the clocks.

I play …
at … o'clock.

I have breakfast at …
I have lunch at …
I have dinner at …

I get up at …

I do my homework at …

I feed my …
at …

I go to
bed
at …

I go to
school at …

Den eigenen Tagesablauf schriftlich beschreiben und vorlesen, Uhrzeiten auf Zifferblättern ergänzen ▸ S. 190

Keli and the dingo

1 Read and write the sentences.

Sorry, just kidding! • Not now, I'm washing the clothes. • Come on, Father, play with me. • A dingo!

Keli fordert seinen Vater auf, mit ihm zu spielen.

Kelis Schwester sagt, dass sie gerade Wäsche wäscht.

Keli warnt vor einem Dingo.

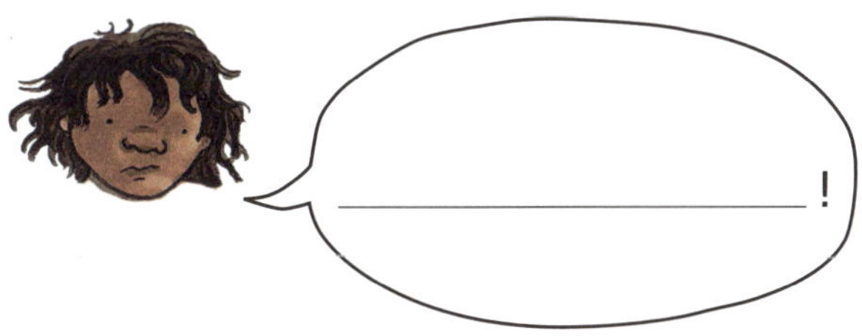

Keli entschuldigt sich und sagt, dass es nur Spaß war.

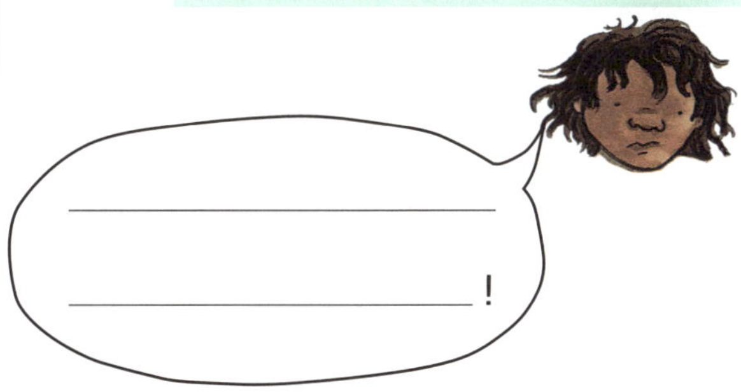

2 Read and act out with two partners.

The Australian Outback

1 Read and write the words.

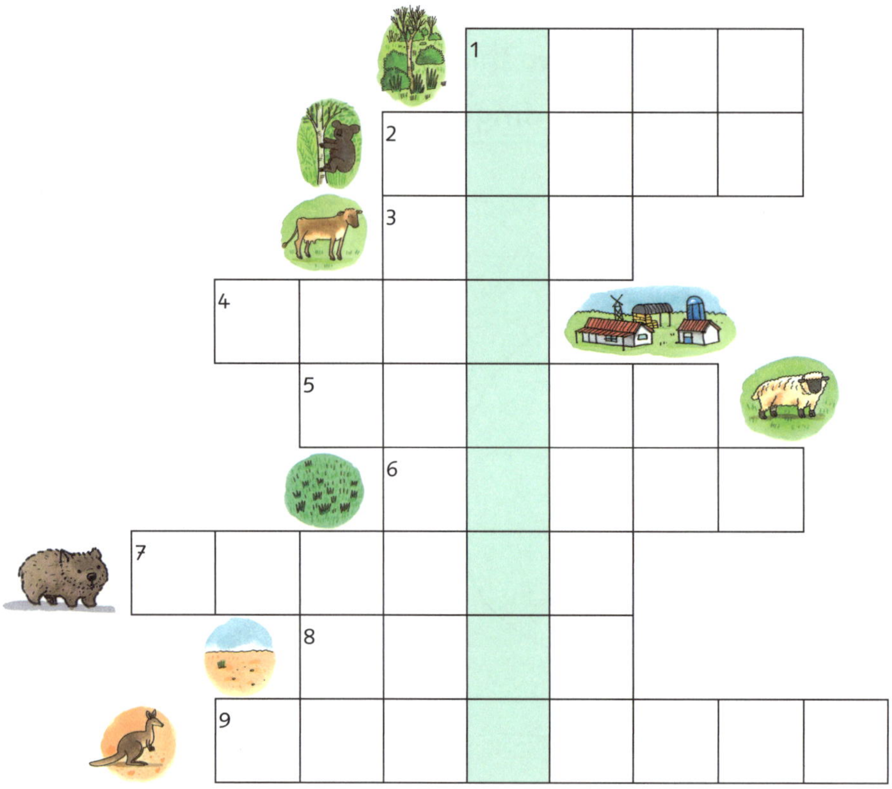

bush
cow
farm
grass
kangaroo
koala
sand
sheep
wombat

It's a ______________________________ .

2 Read and write the rhyming words.

~~bingo~~ • brother • dingo • fun • hand • kangaroo • mother • sand • shoe • stone • sun • telephone

 → bingo ______________________

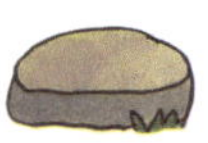 → ______________________

 → ______________________

______________________ ← 

______________________ ← 

______________________ ← 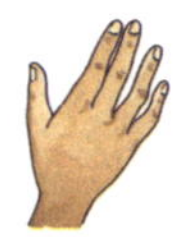

Wörter lesen und ein Kreuzworträtsel lösen; Reimwörter finden und aufschreiben ▸ S. 198

Portfolio: My favourite animal in Australia

1 Draw or glue your favourite animal.

a dingo

a wombat

a snake

an emu

a koala

a spider

a kangaroo

2 Write about your animal.

Was ich dazugelernt habe

Datum: ____________________

Zeige jetzt noch einmal, was du kannst.
Ich fand die Aufgabe: ☺ leicht 😐 mittel ☹ schwer

◯ **1** Ich habe das Lied gesungen, die Chants und den Reim gesprochen:
The Kookaburra Song ☐ On the train ☐ Kangaroo shoe ☐
Let's pack the schoolbag ☐

◯ **2** Ich habe (Name) ____________________ die Tiere genannt:

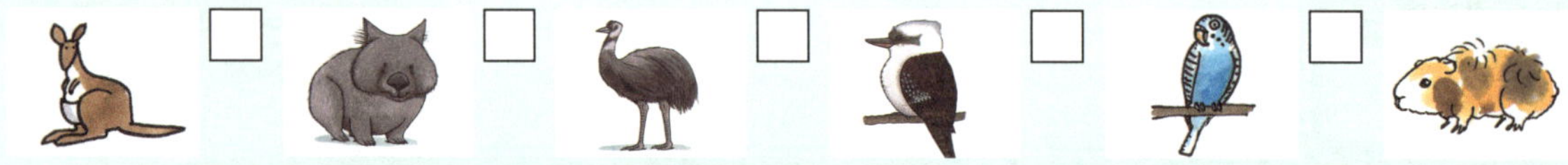

Ich kann einige davon aufschreiben: ______________________________

____

◯ **3** Ich habe (Name) ____________________ ein  oder einen  beschrieben. ☐

◯ **4** (Name) ____________________ und ich haben uns gegenseitig Anweisungen gegeben und diese ausgeführt. ☐

◯ **5** Ich habe (Name) ____________________ die Uhrzeiten gesagt ☐ und was ich zu diesen Tageszeiten mache ☐:

Buses in South Africa

1 What's on top of the buses? Read the sentences. Write the numbers.

Bus number 8: There are two bikes, one chair, five bags and one table on top of the bus.

Bus number 11: There is one bed, two bikes, two chairs and five bags on top of the bus.

Bus number 13: There are two beds, five bags, one table and two bikes on top of the bus.

2 What's on top of buses number 15, 17 and 20? Write.

Bus number 15: There ______________________________

______________________________ on top of the bus.

Bus number 17: ______________________________

______________________________.

Bus number 20: ______________________________

______________________________.

Where's the clinic?

CD 2.14

1 Listen. Complete the dialogue.

and then turn left • the clinic • Thank you • You're welcome • Where's the clinic

Excuse me, please.

______________________________?

Dr. Heal möchte wissen, wo das Krankenhaus ist.

Go straight on ______________________________.

There's ______________________________.

Der Mann antwortet, dass sie zuerst geradeaus gehen und dann links abbiegen soll. Dort befindet sich das Krankenhaus.

______________________________!

Dr. Heal bedankt sich.

______________________________.

Der Mann antwortet, dass er gern geholfen hat.

2 Write a dialogue with your partner. Read.

Excuse me, please. • Go to • Thank you. • You're welcome. • Where's • Turn left. • Turn right. • Go straight on. • the tree • the river • the house • the school • the clinic • Nombeko's house

____

____

______________________________.

____

____

____

______________________________.

______________________________.

______________________________.

Einen Hörtext verstehen und einen Dialog dementsprechend schriftlich vervollständigen; einen Dialog schreiben und mit einem Partner vorlesen ▸ S. 208

I'm not well

CD 2.22 **1** Listen to the dialogues. ✓ **2** Read. Tick the correct answer.

1		2		3	
I'm not hungry.	☐	No, I'm sad.	☐	Go to bed.	☐
I'm hungry.	☐	No, I'm well.	☐	Go to the clinic.	☐
I'm angry.	☐	No, I'm not well.	☐	Go home.	☐

3 Complete the speech bubbles. Read.

a cold • a cough • an earache • a headache • a sore throat • a tummy ache

I've got ______________
______________.

I've got ______________
______________.

____
______________.

____
______________.

____
______________.

____
______________.

Dialoge hören und verstehen, entsprechende Sätze abhaken;
Sätze vervollständigen, schreiben und vorlesen ▸ S. 213/214

What's wrong with you?

1 Circle 8 more words. **2** Write the words.

X	H	B	C	D	E	F	F	C	cough
M	E	D	I	C	I	N	E	O	
E	A	R	A	C	H	E	E	L	
Q	D	O	C	T	O	R	S	D	
O	A	S	L	G	J	R	U	S	
M	C	T	I	K	C	L	L	Y	
W	H	D	N	U	R	S	E	H	
B	E	D	I	Z	R	E	T	A	
D	N	K	C	O	U	G	H	M	

3 Complete the speech bubbles. **4** Read with a partner.

Wörter in einem Rätsel finden und diese aufschreiben;
Minidialoge vervollständigen bzw. schreiben und mit einem Partner lesen ▸ S. 216

What's on the tree?

1 Sort and write the words.

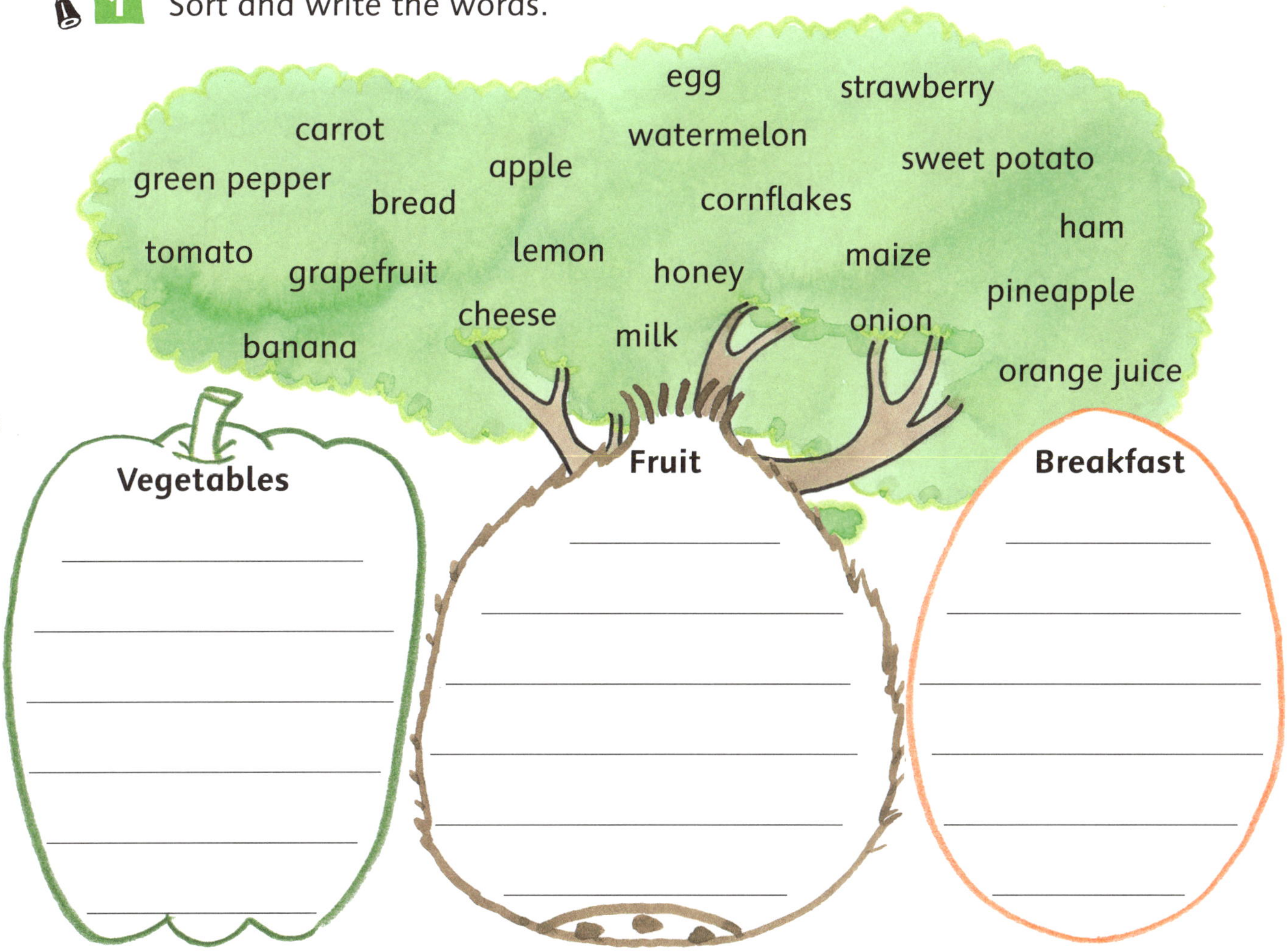

2 How often do you eat the food from number 1? Write.

1 ______________________________

2 ______________________________

3 ______________________________

4 ______________________________

Wörter nach Wortfeldern ordnen;
sagen und aufschreiben, wie oft man bestimmte Lebensmittel isst, die Sätze vorlesen ▸ S. 218

Portfolio: My check-up

EARS • EYES • FEET • FITNESS

1 Fill in your check-up card.

2 Talk about your check-up.

Name: ______________________________ Date: ______________

HEIGHT

I'm __________ metre ________ .

____

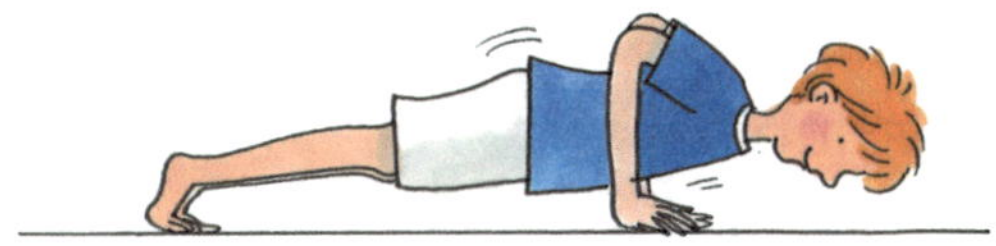

I can do ________ out of 5 press-ups.

☐ very good
☐ good
☐ not so good

5 very good
2–4 good
0–1 not so good

______

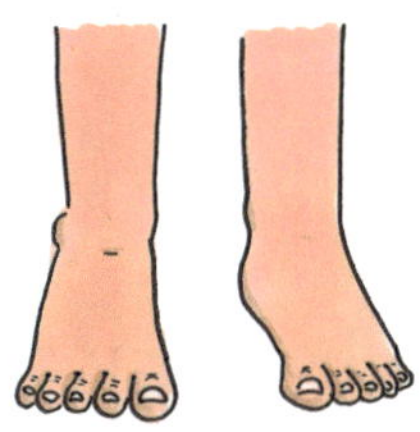

My right foot is __________ centimetres long.

My left foot is __________ centimetres long.

______

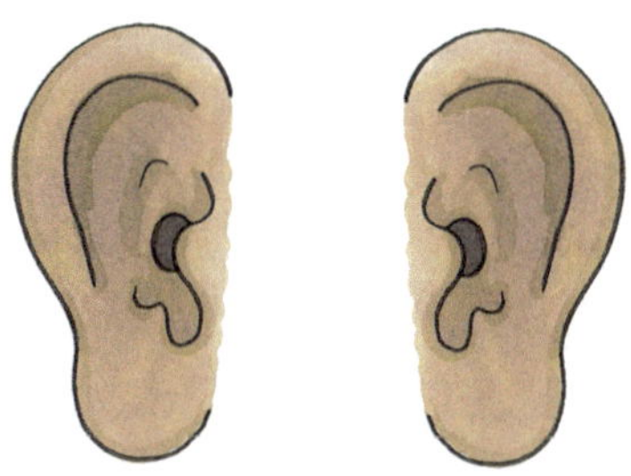

______ out of 3

☐ very good
☐ good
☐ not so good

3 very good
2 good
0–1 not so good

______

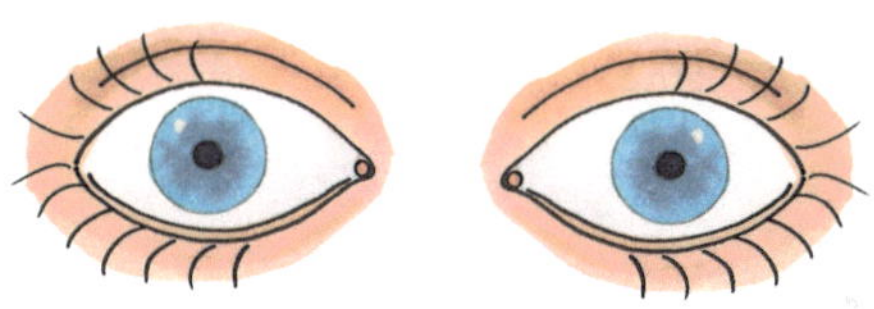

______ out of 9

☐ very good
☐ good
☐ not so good

7–9 very good
4–6 good
0–3 not so good

Was ich dazugelernt habe

Datum: ____________________

Zeige jetzt noch einmal, was du kannst.

Ich fand die Aufgabe: ☺ leicht 😐 mittel ☹ schwer

◯ **1** Ich habe das Lied gesungen und den Reim gesprochen:

The ABC song ☐ My headache is bad ☐

ABCD
EFGHIJKL
MNOPQR
STUVW
XYZ

◯ **2** Ich habe (Name) ____________________ meinen Namen auf Englisch buchstabiert. ☐

◯ **3** Ich habe (Name) ____________________ gesagt, mit welchen Zahlen die Krankheiten nummeriert werden sollen. Ich habe das fehlende Wort für die Krankheit aufgeschrieben.

☐ ☐ ☐ ☐ ☐ ☐

☐ headache ☐ tummy ache ☐ sore throat

☐ cough ☐ earache ☐ ____________________

◯ **4** Ich habe (Name) ____________________ die Namen von ____ Obst- und Gemüsesorten genannt und kann mein Lieblingsgemüse und meine Lieblingsfrucht aufschreiben.

My favourite vegetable is ____________________

My favourite fruit is ____________________

◯ **5** Ich habe (Name) ____________________ gesagt, wie groß ich bin und wie lang mein Fuß ist. ☐

Ich habe verstanden, wie groß (Name) ____________________ ist und wie groß ihr/sein Fuß ist.

___ metre ____ tall

____ centimetres long

People everywhere

People • People there •
can I sit • can I stand •
can you move a bit • here

1 Write and read the rhyme.

People ____________. ______________________________.

______________________ everywhere.

Where ______________________?

Where ______________________?

Excuse me, please, ______________________________?

Hira's house

1 Talk about Hira's house.

CD 2.28 **2** Listen. Number the rooms.

3 Complete the speech bubbles. Upstairs or downstairs?

4 Write. Where are the things?

There's a computer in Adi's bedroom.

____

____

____

blue chair
~~computer~~
poster
toilet
TV
wardrobe

Die Abbildung beschreiben; einem Hörtext Informationen entnehmen und die Zimmer entsprechend nummerieren; Sätze vervollständigen; aufschreiben, in welchem Zimmer sich die Dinge befinden ▸ S. 229

Who is it?

1 Read the sentences. Draw a picture of a girl or boy in your class.

2 Write about the girl or boy. Read the text.

His name is Adi.

Her name is Maya.

He's short.

She's tall.

He has got blond hair.

She has got black hair.

He has got green eyes.

She has got brown eyes.

He has got a red T-shirt on.

She has got a yellow pullover and blue trousers on.

______ name is ______

He has got glasses.

She has got freckles.

Market stands

1 Talk about the market stands.

2 Read and write what you can buy.

bananas • books • carpets • computer games • dresses • glasses • grapefruit • mobile phones • oranges • potatoes • pumpkins • radios • rice • sandals • skirts • trousers • T-shirts • watches

1

You can buy ____________________

____________________.

2

You ____________________

____________________.

3

____

____________________.

4

____

____________________.

3 Listen to the CD.

CD 2.33

4 Draw. Write the words and numbers.

Hira → [sandals] sandals → 3

Janak → ☐ ____________________ → ☐

Ginger → ☐ ____________________ → ☐

Ravi → ☐ ____________________ → ☐

Maya → ☐ ____________________ → ☐

Adi/Amar → ☐ ____________________ → ☐

Sagen und schreiben, was man an den Marktständen kaufen kann; einem Hörtext Informationen entnehmen und diese aufschreiben ▸ S. 236

Portfolio: My market stand

1 Draw what you can buy at your market stand.

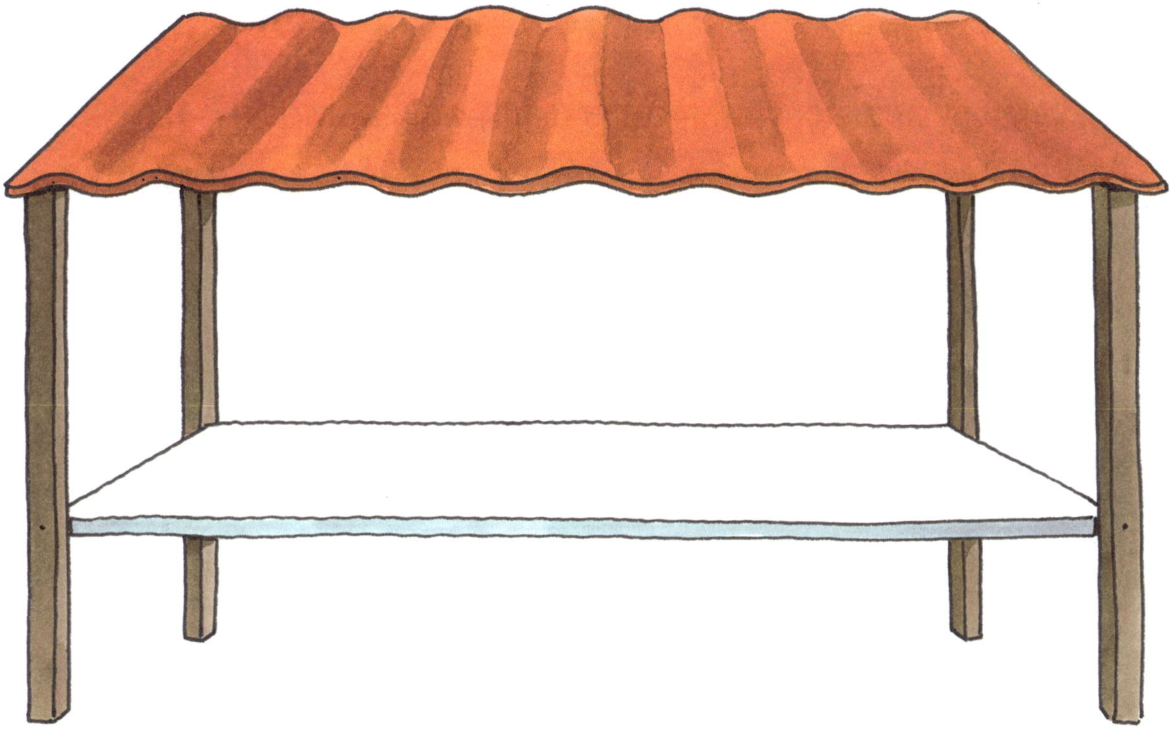

2 Write what you can buy at your market stand.

Zeichnen und aufschreiben, was man auf einem Markt kaufen kann ▸ S. 238

Was ich dazugelernt habe

Datum: ______________________

Zeige jetzt noch einmal, was du kannst.
Ich fand die Aufgabe: ☺ leicht 😐 mittel ☹ schwer

◯ **1** Ich habe das Lied gesungen und den Reim gesprochen:
Loud and busy market ☐ People everywhere ☐

◯ **2** Ich habe (Name) ______________________ ein Zimmer in Hiras Haus beschrieben. ☐

◯ **3** Ich habe (Name) ______________________ gesagt, was ich gern im Fernsehen sehe.
I like to watch films ☐ cartoons ☐ music shows ☐
quiz shows ☐ sports ☐ animal programmes ☐

◯ **4** Ich habe ein Kind aus der Klasse beschrieben.
(Name) ______________________ hat erraten, wer es ist. ☐

◯ **5** Ich habe (Name) ______________________ gesagt, was man auf einem Markt kaufen kann. ☐ Ich habe ________ unterschiedliche Dinge aufgezählt.
Einige davon kann ich auch aufschreiben:

____

____

◯ **6** Ich habe mit (Name) ______________________ ein Einkaufsgespräch geführt. ☐

Christmas lists

1 Talk. Read Ginger's letter to Father Christmas.

2 Write your letter to Father Christmas.

Hiding Easter eggs

1 Talk about the picture. Read.

Is your Easter egg under the tree?

Yes, it is. / No, it isn't.

2 Play the game.

You need: 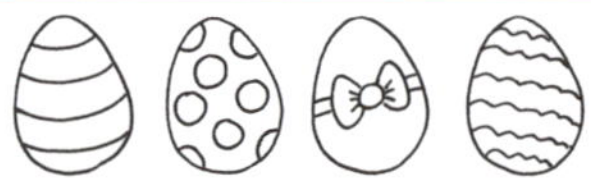

	bush	grass	tree	stones	basket	flowers
in						
under						
behind						

3 Glue your Easter eggs in the garden.
Colour in. Write about your Easter eggs.

Sich zu einer Abbildung äußern, Sätze lesen, ein Spiel spielen; aufschreiben, wo die Ostereier versteckt sind ▸ S. 250

Portfolio: A goodbye show programme

1 Read the programme.

CD 2.44 123 **2** Listen to the CD. Number the acts.

Orange Island

A programme

- ☐ Chant: On Monday no cornflakes
- ☐ Information: We went to Orange Island
- ☐ Portfolio: My fun food
- ☐ Role-play: Two scoops of chocolate ice cream, please
- [1] Saying welcome: We went on a trip around the world
- ☐ Song: Oranges, tasty oranges
- ☐ Song: Travelling the world

3 Write the name of the country and your programme.
Who is in the act? Write the names.

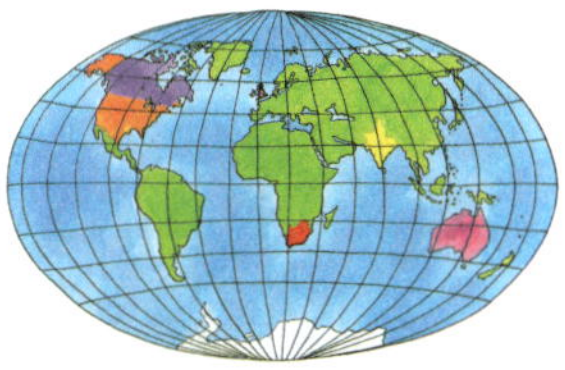

Our programme

______________________	______________________ name(s)
______________________	______________________ name(s)
______________________	______________________ name(s)
______________________	______________________ name(s)
______________________	______________________ name(s)
______________________	______________________ name(s)
______________________	______________________ name(s)

Programmpunkte lesen und in eine gehörte Reihenfolge bringen;
ein Programm für die *Goodbye show* mit den Namen der Akteure schreiben ▸ S. 257/258

Portfolio: My favourites

1 Talk about the pictures. Read. **2** Write about your favourites.

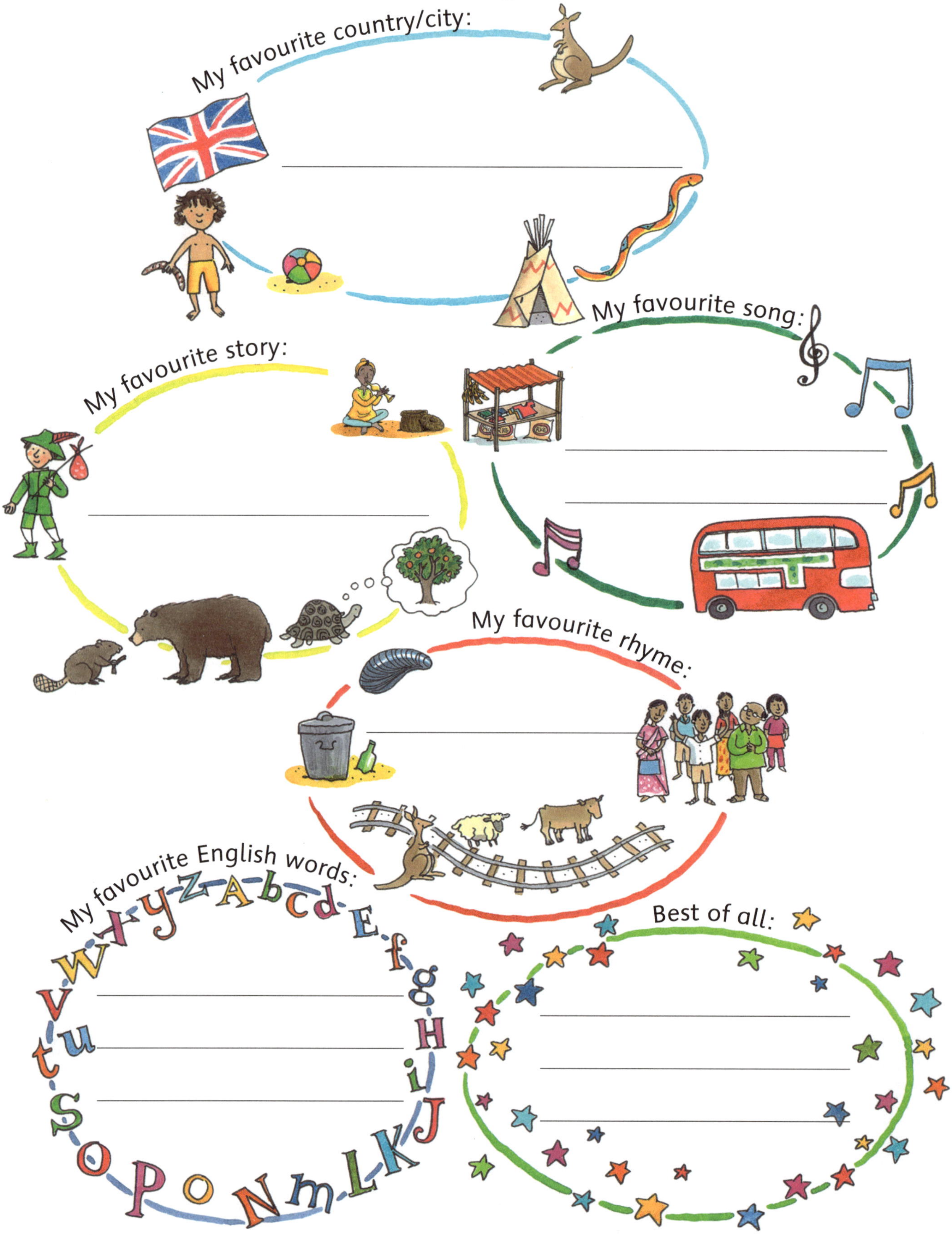

Über seine Highlights aus Klasse 4 sprechen und diese aufschreiben ▸ S. 261/262

Our presentation

1 Read the sentences. Talk.

Speak loudly. • Look at the class. •
Speak clearly. • Listen to the rhyme. •
Let's sing a song. • Stand straight.

2 Complete the speech bubbles.

1

Sage, dass alle ein Lied singen sollen.

2

Fordere alle auf, sich den Reim anzuhören.

3

Bitte jemanden, laut zu sprechen.

4

Sage, dass das Kind gerade stehen soll.

5

Fordere jemanden auf, deutlich zu sprechen.

6

Sage, dass das Kind die Klasse anschauen soll.

London sights

Adjectives

Beach

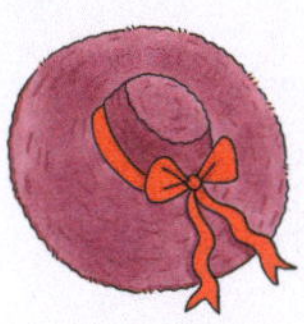

Word fields

Activities on the beach

Camping

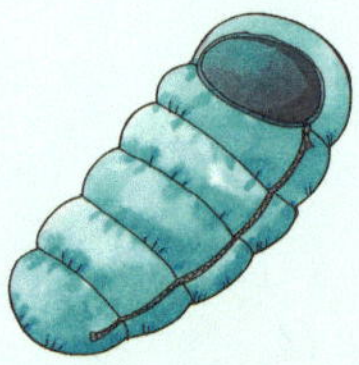

Pets

Months

1 January ____________

2 ____________

3 ____________

4 ____________

5 ____________

6 ____________

7 ____________

8 ____________

9 ____________

10 ____________

11 ____________

12 ____________

Activities at school

____

____

____

____

____

____

____

____

____

____

____

____

Illnesses

Fruit and vegetables

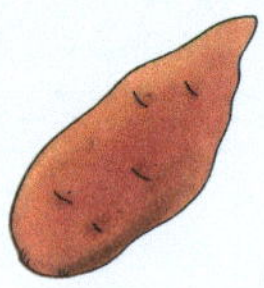

TV programmes

At the market

Word list

A

a ein, eine
a lot of viel/e
a quarter past/to viertel nach/vor
about über
act Akt, Aufführung
action Action, Handlung
activity Aktivität
adjective Adjektiv
afternoon Nachmittag
again wieder, noch einmal
agree sich einig sein, zustimmen
all alle
all right in Ordnung
already schon
American football American Football
angry wütend
animal Tier
animal programme Tiersendung
anything etwas
April April
are sind
arm Arm
at bei, im, um
August August
aunt Tante
Australia Australien

B

back zurück
badminton Federball/Badminton (Spiel)
badminton birdie der Federball
bag Tasche
banana Banane
barrel Fass
baseball Baseball
basket Korb
basketball Basketball
bathroom Badezimmer
be sein
beach Strand
beach ball Wasserball
beach towel Strandtuch
beak Schnabel
bear Bär
beaver Biber
because weil
bed Bett
bedroom Schlafzimmer
behind hinter
bell Glocke
best boy Assistent (Beleuchtung)
between zwischen
big groß
bike Fahrrad
bikini Bikini
bird Vogel
birdie Federball
birdcage Vogelkäfig
birthday Geburtstag
black schwarz
blond blond
blow up sprengen, explodieren
blue blau
body Körper
book Buch
bonfire Lagerfeuer
boomerang Bumerang
boring langweilig
bottle Flasche
bowl Schale
box Kasten
boy Junge
break Pause
breakfast Frühstück
bridge Brücke
British britisch
brown braun
budgie Wellensittich
buffalo Büffel
bus Bus
bus stop Bushaltestelle
bush Strauch, Busch
busy beschäftigt
but aber
buy kaufen
by (go by bus) mit (mit dem Bus fahren)

C

camera Kamera, Fotoapparat
camera man Kameramann
camp Lager, Camp
camping Zelten
camping store Campinggeschäft
can können
Canada Kanada
car Auto
card Karte
careful vorsichtig
carpet Teppich
carrot Mohrrübe
cartoon Zeichentrickfilm
cat Katze
cave Höhle
CD player CD-Spieler
centimetre Zentimeter
chair Stuhl
cheese Käse
chicken Huhn
child Kind
children Kinder
chimney Kamin, Schornstein
Christmas Weihnachten
city Stadt
clapper Materialassistent (Kamera)
class Klasse
clean saubermachen
clear klar, deutlich
climb klettern
clinic Klinik
clock Uhr
clothes Kleidung
coconut Kokosnuss
coin Münze
cold 1. kalt 2. Erkältung
collect sammeln
colour 1. Farbe 2. (aus)malen
colour in ausmalen
coloured pencil Buntstift
come kommen
come up aufgehen (Sonne)
comic Comic(heft)
computer Computer
computer game Computerspiel
cookie Keks
corner Ecke
correct richtig
cough Husten
count zählen
counter Spielstein
country Land
cow Kuh
crayon Stift
crocodile Krokodil
crocus Krokus
cross überqueren
cut off abschneiden

D

dad Papa
daffodil Narzisse
dangerous gefährlich
day Tag
December Dezember
dice Würfel
dingo Dingo
dinner Abendessen
director Regisseur, Chef
do machen
doctor Arzt/Ärztin
dog Hund
dollar Dollar
down herunter, unten
downstairs unten
draw zeichnen
dream Traum
drink trinken
duck Ente

E

eagle Adler
earache Ohrenschmerzen
Easter Ostern
Easter egg Osterei
eat essen
egg Ei
eighty achtzig
elephant Elefant
else sonst, sonst noch
emu Emu
enjoy genießen
envelope Briefumschlag
every jede/r/s
everybody alle
excuse entschuldigen
eye Auge

F

family Familie
famous berühmt
farm Bauernhof, Farm
fast schnell
father Vater
Father Christmas Weihnachtsmann
February Februar
feed füttern
feet Füße
fifty fünfzig
film Film
film crew Filmteam
find finden
find out herausfinden
finish 1. Schluss 2. aufhören, beenden
fireworks Feuerwerk
fish Fisch
fitness Fitness
flag Flagge
flower Blume
flute Flöte
fly fliegen
fold falten
food Essen
foot Fuß
football Fußball
for für
forget vergessen
forty vierzig
freckle Sommersprosse
free frei, kostenlos
friend Freund/in
from von
fruit Obst
full voll
full of voller
fun Spaß
funny lustig

G

Germany Deutschland
get werden, bekommen
get up aufstehen
giraffe Giraffe
girl Mädchen
give geben
glass Glas
glasses Brille
glue 1. Kleber 2. kleben
go gehen
go camping zelten gehen
go down untergehen
gold Gold
good gut
goose Gans
grandpa Opa
grass Gras
Great Britain Großbritannien
green grün
greeting Gruß
ground Boden
guinea pig Meerschweinchen
gunpowder Schießpulver
guy Kerl

H

hair Haar
half halb
half past eine halbe Stunde nach
hamburger Hamburger
hamster Hamster
happy glücklich
have got haben
has got hat
have haben
have a picnic picknicken
have breakfast frühstücken
have dinner zu Abend essen
have lunch zu Mittag essen
head Kopf
headache Kopfschmerzen
height Höhe, Größe
hello Hallo
help helfen
helper Helfer
her ihr/e
here hier
his sein/e
hole Loch
holidays Ferien
home Haus, Zuhause
homework Hausaufgaben
honey Honig
hoof Huf
hop hüpfen
hope hoffen
hot heiß
house Haus
how wie
hundred hundert
hungry hungrig

I

I ich
idea Idee
illness Krankheit
in in
in front of vor
India Indien
information Information
instruction Anweisung
interesting interessant
into in (… hinein)
is ist
it es

J

January Januar
job Arbeit
July Juli
jump hüpfen
June Juni
just nur

K

kangaroo Känguru
kill töten
kitchen Küche
kite Drachen
knee Knie
know wissen, kennen
koala Koala
kookaburra Kookaburra

L

lake See
left links
leg Bein
lesson Schulstunde, Lektion
let lassen
letter 1. Brief, 2. Buchstabe
light Licht
like mögen
line 1. Reihe, Zeile 2. Linie
listen (to) zuhören
live leben
living room Wohnzimmer
long lang
look schauen, sehen
look at something sich etwas ansehen
loud laut
luck Glück
lunch Mittagessen

M

magazine Zeitschrift
maize Mais
make machen
man Mann
map Landkarte
March März
market Markt
market stand Marktstand
May Mai
me mich, mir
meet treffen
medicine Medizin
melon Melone
message Nachricht
metre Meter
microphone Mikrofon
mine mein, meiner, meines
minute Minute
mobile phone Handy
money Geld
monkey Affe
month Monat
moose Elch
morning Morgen
mother Mutter
mountain Berg
mouse 1. Maus 2. Computermaus
mouth Mund
move bewegen
much viel
mud Schlamm
mum Mama
music Musik
music show Musiksendung

N

name Name
narrator Erzähler
never nie
new neu
next nächster, nächste
next to bei, neben
nice schön, nett
night Nacht
ninety neunzig
nose Nase
not nicht
November November
now jetzt
number 1. Nummer 2. nummerieren
nurse Krankenschwester

O

o'clock Uhr
October Oktober
old alt
on an, auf
onion Zwiebel
only nur
on top oben, auf
on top of über
open 1. öffnen, 2. offen
ostrich Vogel Strauß
our unser, unsere
out of aus, von
over über

P

page Seite
palace Palast
paper Papier
paper cup Pappbecher
paper towel Papierhandtuch
past nach
peanut Erdnuss
peanut butter Erdnussbutter
pen Füller
pencil Bleistift
pencil case Federmappe
pencil sharpener Bleistiftspitzer
penny/pence Penny/Pence (englische Münze)
people Menschen, Leute
pet Haustier
picnic Picknick
picture Bild
pineapple Ananas
pirate Pirat
play spielen
player Spieler
please bitte
plot Verschwörung
plotter Verschwörer
pocketbook Taschenbuch
pocket knife Taschenmesser
police officer Polizist
poor arm
postcard Postkarte
pot Kanne, Topf
potato Kartoffel
pound Pfund
presentation Präsentation
press-up Liegestütz
programme Programm

Word list

puddle Pfütze
put setzen, stellen, legen

Q

quarter viertel
queen Königin
quiz show Ratesendung

R

rabbit Kaninchen
rat Ratte
read lesen
ready fertig
red rot
red pepper rote Paprika
reindeer Rentier
remember erinnern
repeat wiederholen
rhyme Reim
rice Reis
rich reich
right rechts
river Fluss
rock Stein
role-play Rollenspiel
roll rollen
roof Dach
room Zimmer
royal königlich
rubber Radiergummi
rubbish Abfall
rucksack Rucksack
ruler Lineal
run rennen
rupee Rupie

S

sad traurig
sand Sand
sandal Sandale
sandcastle Sandburg
say sagen
school Schule
scissors Schere
sea Meer
seashell Muschel
seat Sitz, Platz
see sehen
sentence Satz
September September
seventy siebzig
shark Hai
sheep Schaf/e
shirt Hemd
shoe Schuh
shop Geschäft, Laden
shop assistant Verkäufer/-in
short 1. kurz 2. klein
shoulder Schulter
show Aufführung
sight Sehenswürdidkeit
sister Schwester
sixty sechzig
skirt Rock
sleep schlafen
sleeping bag Schlafsack
sleepy schläfrig
sleigh Schlitten
small klein
snow Schnee
sock Socke
sofa Sofa
soldier Soldat
some etwas
something etwas
sometimes manchmal
song Lied
soon bald
sore throat Halsschmerzen
sound operator Toningenieur
sour cream Sauerrahm
South Africa Südafrika
speak sprechen
sports Sport
sports programme Sportsendung
stamp Briefmarke
stand stehen
start 1. Beginn, Anfang 2. beginnen, anfangen
station Bahnhof
stone Stein
stop 1. stoppen, aufhören, 2. Haltestelle
storeroom Vorratskammer
straight gerade
straight on geradeaus
street Straße
strong stark
sun Sonne
sunglasses Sonnenbrille
sun hat Sonnenhut
sweet potato Süßkartoffel
swim schwimmen
swimmer Schwimmer
swimming trunks Badehose

T

table tennis Tischtennis
tail Schwanz
take nehmen
take off ausziehen
tall groß
tea Tee
teepee Tipi
tent Zelt
text Text
text message SMS
that der, die, das
the der, die, das
there dort
they sie (Mehrzahl)
thirty dreißig
think denken
throw werfen
tick abhaken
ticket Fahrschein
ticket machine Fahrkartenautomat
time Zeit
timetable Stundenplan
tired müde
to nach, zu
toe Zeh
toilet Toilette
top oben
torch Taschenlampe
tortoise Schildkröte
touch berühren
town Stadt
track Spur
train Zug
travel reisen
treason Verrat
treasure chest Schatzkiste
tree Baum
trousers Hose
tulip Tulpe
tummy Bauch
tummy ache Bauchweh
turn abbiegen, umdrehen
turn around umdrehen, wenden
TV Fernseher
twenty-one einundzwanzig
twin Zwilling

U

uncle Onkel
under unter
underground 1. unter der Erde, 2. U-Bahn
underline unterstreichen
up oben, auf, herauf
upstairs oben
USA Vereinigte Staaten von Amerika

V

vegetable Gemüse
very sehr
visit 1. Besuch, 2. besuchen
volleyball Volleyball

W

walk gehen
want wollen, möchten
watch 1. Armbanduhr 2. zusehen, zuschauen
water Wasser
water bottle Wasserflasche
watermelon Wassermelone
we wir
wear anhaben, tragen
week Woche
welcome 1. Willkommen, 2. begrüßen
well gesund, gut
what was
where wo, wohin
white weiß
who wer
why warum
with mit
wolf Wolf
wombat Wombat
word Wort
world Welt
world map Weltkarte
write schreiben
wrong falsch

Y

year Jahr
yellow gelb
your dein
Yuck! Igitt!